Reimagining the Seven Deadly Sins

Reshaping Our Hearts in a Complex World

James Philipps

TWENTY-THIRD PUBLICATIONS
twentythirdpublications.com

Twenty-Third Publications
One Montauk Avenue, Suite 200
New London, CT 06320
(860) 437-3012 or (800) 321-0411
www.twentythirdpublications.com

Cover photo: Shutterstock.com / Billion Photos

ISBN: 978-1-62785-527-3
Printed in the U.S.A.

bayard A division of Bayard, Inc.

DEDICATION

To JennaLynn, Stephen, Joseph,
Maggie, Robbie, Christopher,
Georgina, Michael, Ryan,
Erik, Joe, and Alicia

who hold the potential for a glorious future
in their hearts, minds, and hands.

CONTENTS

ACKNOWLEDGMENTS

Thanks to Kathy Hendricks for shepherding this book through the editorial process.

Thanks to Dan Connors for his usual attention to both the big picture and the details.

Thanks to Michelle Gerstel and Jeff McCall for proofreading and preparing this manuscript for publication.

Finally, my ongoing thanks to Kerry Moriarty for being the best author liaison a writer could ask for.

INTRODUCTION

The idea for this book began with an apple. Not the metaphorical kind we sometimes imagine in the story of Adam and Eve. A real apple, one that I was about to eat as part of my lunch as I sat at my desk between classes. I had just finished teaching a lesson in social justice, which, combined with a few minutes of quiet, probably gave rise to the following reflections.

As I looked at the apple, I thought about all of the people who stood between me and the orchard whence the apple came. Likely that orchard was in Washington State, where the vast majority of apples in the United States originate. There were the grower who owned the orchard, the migrant workers who picked the apples, the workers who maintained the orchard and prepared the fruit for shipping. A bit further on down the chain are those who pack the trucks that deliver the apples to market at the various distribution centers, the drivers themselves, and, nearer to me, the owner of the supermarket here in the eastern suburbs of New York City and those who stock the shelves and handle the cash registers where I bought the apple on my weekly shopping trip. That's a great many people working very hard—and sometimes under deplorable conditions—so that I could have my lunch.

Upon further reflection, it occurred to me that when Jesus said, "love your neighbor as you love yourself," the neighborhood wasn't nearly as large and complex as it is today. The world that Jesus in his human nature knew was one in which most people made their living as subsistence farmers, closely tied to the land and to one another. Which is not to say that people always treated each other well, but the steps between the grower and the consumer were far fewer, if they even existed at all. Increasingly as our lives in our modern post-industrial society grow ever busier and we become more and more interconnected with people we will never meet, two questions become more and more imperative and demand answers: How do we show the love of Christ in meaningful ways not only to those in our immediate—and relatively tiny—circle of friends, family, and acquaintances but also to those sisters and brothers whose labor we depend on but who live far outside that circle? And what is our responsibility to change the unjust social systems that oppress them while benefiting us?

These two questions lie at the core of Catholic social justice teaching, a body of instruction and inspiration that, in its modern form, dates back to Pope Leo XIII in the late nineteenth century. And while most Catholics have a glancing knowledge of some key points—certainly the right to life and possibly the preferential option for the poor—many of the faithful have not yet made a fundamental shift in head and heart that is essential if Catholicism is to be a relevant and dynamic moral force in the twenty-first century and beyond. It is the recognition that while it is still important to keep one's personal house in order by following the Ten Commandments and Jesus' exhortations in the Sermon on the Mount, focusing only on our personal sins and our personal journey toward holiness will not be sufficient. If we are to truly be disciples of Christ and stand up to the massive social injustice in our world, as he did in his, we must care at least as much about the state of the world as we do the state of our individual souls. Collectively, the body of Christ must be the "thermostat" Dr. Martin Luther King Jr. calls us to be, setting the moral temperature of society, and not merely a "thermometer" that mimics within the Church the same standard of morality—and immorality—of the world.

What might such a shift in perspective look like? The purpose of this book is to offer an example, using the lens of the seven deadly sins, but focusing not so much on the ways they are manifested in individual behavior as on the way they deform with all their ugliness the underpinnings of modern society. What does the sin of greed look like, for example, when we focus not on the individual thief but on the ways in which the privileged few tilt the playing field so that the law protects their rapacious grasping for more at the expense of those simply struggling to feed, clothe, and house their families?

In part 1, the focus will be on what this fundamental shift in emphasis looks like. We begin with Jesus as a model of how to identify personal and social sin and keep them in the right balance. Chapter 2 provides a brief review of basic Catholic teaching about conscience and proper conscience formation, especially how both pertain to and are affected by social injustice. Chapter 3 concludes this basic overview by going into more detail about the "new things" Pope Leo XIII noticed in his groundbreaking encyclical, *Rerum Novarum*, and why Pope Leo's letter challenged the fundamental approach to moral theology in the Church.

Part 2 of the book focuses on the seven deadly sins directly, beginning with a brief review of what these sins are and why they are so particularly deadly. After that we take a closer look at each of the sins and apply them to particular social injustices of our day. In chapter 5, we'll look at how the sins of pride (arrogance) and lust provide the poisonous soil for the two fundamental sins of American society—racism and sexism. Chapter 6 looks at the connection between greed, gluttony, and sloth and the gaping global economic inequalities of our planet as well as their contribution to the degradation of the natural environment, in particular in relation to climate change. The final chapter of the book focuses on how wrath and envy cause the epidemic of gun violence in America as well as the demonization of the immigrant.

Just when things seem darkest, the book's conclusion offers a few reasons why we should not be afraid to venture out into the farthest regions of this enormous global neighborhood. Why, in fact, divine grace may have led us to this particular crossroads at this particular time. It seems we are faced on all sides with an inescapable and stark choice. To slightly paraphrase Pope Francis, that choice is whether to build bridges of understanding and compassion or walls of hate and fear.

Along the way, at the end of every chapter, the building materials for those magnificent bridges are supplied in the form of readings from both Scripture and literature, inviting the reader to think deeply and prayerfully about the possibilities. And if we are willing to be people of prayer and people of courage, standing in solidarity in Christ, within whom "we live and move and have our being" as St. Paul wrote, then we will not only beat our swords into plowshares but also level our walls and turn them into bridges.

PART I

Recognizing Social Sin

CHAPTER 1

"WHERE'S THE GUY?"

Adopting the perspective of Jesus

The scribes and the Pharisees brought a woman who had been caught in adultery; and making her stand before all of them, they said to him, "Teacher, this woman was caught in the very act of committing adultery. Now in the law Moses commanded us to stone such women. Now what do you say?"...When they kept on questioning him, he straightened up and said to them, "Let anyone among you who is without sin be the first to throw a stone at her." And once again he bent down and wrote on the ground. When they heard it, they went away, one by one, beginning with the elders; and Jesus was left alone with the woman standing before him. Jesus straightened up and said to her, "Woman, where are they? Has no one condemned you?" She said, "No one, sir." And Jesus said, "Neither do I condemn you. Go your way, and from now on do not sin again." » **JOHN 8:1–11**

Jesus' actions in the story of the woman caught in adultery would have made Sherlock Holmes proud. The famous detective created by Sir Arthur Conan Doyle solved more than one case that seemed impossible to crack by simply noticing the obvious. In the story of the woman, Jesus too notices the obvious. If a woman is being dragged by herself through the streets into the public square on the grounds of adultery, the obvious question is: "Where's the guy?"

The answer, unfortunately from a modern perspective, is also obvious. In the Mosaic Law that Jesus and all of those in the story followed, the penalty of death by stoning in the case of adultery applied only to the woman caught in the act of adultery. Why? Because according to the patriarchal culture of the day, women were a special class of property belonging to men. The Bible is full of examples of this prejudice; here's one: In their original wording, the ninth and tenth commandments prohibit coveting "thy neighbor's goods" and "thy neighbor's wife." Our modern sensibility encourages us to substitute "spouse," and while that makes sense morally, it changes the original meaning. A man's wife, in biblical times, belonged to him every bit as much as did his material possessions, his children, and his farm animals.

Jesus recognizes this societal assumption as did every other man in that crowd. The difference between Jesus and the elders is that Jesus sees it for the social sin that it is. The others see it as "God's will"—though to say that they would have not on some level recognized it as a convenient way to protect the status of the ruling elites (all of whom were men) would be naive. And so when Jesus says, "Let he who has not sinned cast the first stone," he is not so much speaking of their personal sins; he is speaking of the social injustice in which they are all participating—the dehumanization of women.

PERSONAL SIN VS. SOCIAL SIN

Of course, Jesus recognizes personal sins such as adultery as real dangers. This is why he instructs the woman to "go and sin no more." Jesus knows that all personal sins are against God's will, not because God is a control freak who will not brook disobedience among his children, but because God's will for each of us is that we live lives of joy, and joyful lives are chock full of deep and meaningful relationships. As demonstrated in Genesis chapters 3–11, personal sins act like a sharp knife slashing through the sacred relationships of our lives, causing disharmony between the sinner, the community, nature, and God.

For all the damage personal sin does, however, it pales in comparison to the devastation wrought by social sin. Social sin occurs when a society operates through structures that are oppressive and that undermine human dignity. Social injustice is the effect of social sin. Precisely because they deviate from the norm of what we consider moral behavior, personal sins (at least in the case of sins of commission) can be identified, the sinner can be helped to see the error of their ways, and, if by God's grace there is a genuine desire on the part of the sinner to repent, they can make the necessary changes to behavior and attitude and receive the forgiveness God is eager to supply. Thus the reason the Church considers reconciliation a sacrament.

Social sins, on the other hand, are much more insidious. When the structures of a society are bent away from the "arc of justice," a phrase used often by Dr. Martin Luther King Jr., sin becomes so much a part of our moral environment that we almost stop noticing it. A vicious cycle is set up as the injustices of the society in which we live become a breeding ground for more and more personal sin, which leads to even more injustice. As we will explore in the next chapter, conscience becomes ever more deformed as we gradually lose contact with the moral compass within that seeks to guide us.

There is a reason that the Hebrew prophets were persecuted, rejected, and often killed. There is a reason our modern prophets who speak against the social sins of today suffer such violent rejection. Nelson Mandela, for example, spent twenty-five years in jail for peacefully but persistently opposing apartheid in South Africa. Like the elders in the story of the woman caught in adultery, we lose our sense of real sin, swallowing the camel of our complicity with social injustice while we strain out the gnat of the personal sins of others—but hardly ever our own.

"SEE, I MAKE ALL THINGS NEW!"

The time has come for a paradigm shift. As Pope Leo XIII prophetically pointed out at the end of the nineteenth century, society's increasing complexity since the time of Jesus calls for a drastic reevaluation of how we understand the Commandments and Beatitudes. (We will explore Pope Leo's XIII groundbreaking encyclical, and its implications, in chapter 3.) The "neighborhood" in which we are called to love one another is so much larger, and the vast bulk of it is made up of people we will never meet in person but who will be tremendously affected by the decisions we make in all areas of our lives. (Just take a moment to consider what you had for breakfast this morning or the clothes you are wearing as you read this. How many people were involved in bringing those products to you, beginning with those who grew and harvested the raw materials or who tended the animals?) While the Ten Commandments remain as relevant as ever, Catholic moral teaching increasingly emphasizes our responsibility to reform not just ourselves but our society. In fact, it is simply impossible to do one without the other.

This shift in emphasis takes the form of seven basic themes or principles that, woven together, frame the social justice teaching of the Church. According to the website of the United States Conference of Catholic Bishops (usccb.org), they are:

1) ***The life and dignity of the human person***—Sometimes referred to as the "seamless garment of life," this keystone tenet holds that life is sacred from the moment of conception to the moment of natural death.

2) ***The right to full participation in society***—Human beings by nature are both sacred and social. Every human being must be able to fully access all that is necessary to live a fully human life. These things include food, clothing, and shelter but also less tangible things, such as education and health care.

3) ***Rights and responsibilities***—As proclaimed in the foundational documents of our country, human beings have certain inalienable rights (life, liberty, and the pursuit of happiness) but also corresponding responsibilities to participate in and build a just society.

4) ***The preferential option for the poor***—We must always consider the needs of the poor first in making decisions and allocating resources, which requires us to focus more on the common good than our personal interests.

5) ***The rights and dignity of workers***—this includes things such as a right to a job for all willing to work, a right to a decent wage, a right to safe and decent working conditions, and a right to join a union.

6) ***Solidarity***—A recognition that when Jesus says all are sisters and brothers, he is speaking not metaphorically but literally. As mountain climbers ascending a steep slope tie themselves with rope to one another so that if one slips the rest can support them, we are truly all in this together.

7) ***Care and concern for the environment***—This a principle particularly close to Pope Francis' heart; rather than emphasizing only stewardship—the recognition that human beings are responsible for taking care of the earth for future generations—this principle calls us to recognize our fundamental connection within the web of life of our planet. What we do to mother Earth, we do to ourselves.

THE SOCIAL JUSTICE ARCH

I like to think of these seven principles as a kind of "Social Arch," which I imagine to look something like this:

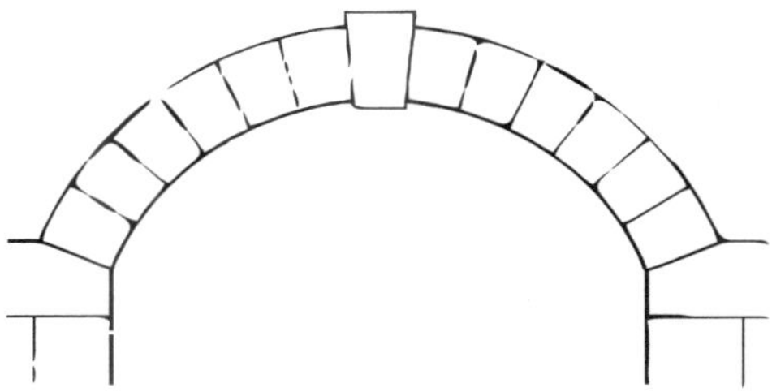

An arch is a support structure; in this case our arch supports a just society. Imagine the keystone, which locks in the other stones, as the dignity of human life; without this recognition no other tenet can stand. Yet to focus only on this principle at the expense of all of the others leaves us with no arch at all. Either all of the principles are observed, or none of them are.

THE SEVEN DEADLY SINS

Centuries ago, the moral teachers of the Church developed a means to simplify many of the requirements of personal morality and discipleship through a prism known as the seven deadly sins. It is no coincidence that both the social justice themes and this list total seven; seven is the number of perfection or completion in the Bible. Follow the seven social justice principles and we are on the way to creating a perfectly just society fully realized in the kingdom of God; indulge in the seven deadly sins and we are on the way to the perfect corruption and radical isolation known as hell.

This is an easy-to-understand means of gaining insight into a fundamental darkness in the human heart that causes us to turn away from joy, refuse God's grace and love, and misuse our free will. A common thread that ties together all seven sins is that each involves an excessive attachment to something that, in and of itself, is good. For example, self-love is a good thing when it is rooted in a recognition that each of us has been created in the image and likeness of God. When we become so attached to our own selfish interests that we ignore the needs of others, however, healthy love of self has been distorted into the sin of pride or arrogance.

The shift toward a greater awareness of social sin has brought to light a fundamental flaw in the traditional way we understand the seven deadly sins. To think of the seven as primarily personal sins suggests that a personal sin is at the root of all of society's evils (not completely untrue, but too simplistic) or that individual salvation is all that matters (I keep my soul clean, and you do as you will). We forget that at the heart of biblical morality is God's desire to save a community, not just a few fortunate individuals. Too many Christians carry around a dangerously flawed perception of salvation that seems to suggest the world around us is a shark-filled ocean and the only safe place to be is on the ark of the Church that floats among the predators. The truth according to Jesus—who instructs his followers to "go and make disciples of all nations"—is closer to the opposite. It is precisely within those shark-infested waters that grace is at work. And if we wish to be caught up in this enterprise of grace, best to jump in and swim with our fellow sinners, having faith that the Spirit will work a transformation in those waters through us. It is what Paul talks about when he calls us to be "in the world, but not of the world."

I invite you, in imitation of Jesus, to look at the obvious as it pertains to the society in which we live and the way its most vulnerable members are treated. Let us together reimagine the seven deadly sins so that we can see not only the excessive attachments of our personal lives but those of the society in which we live and in which we participate and, perhaps most important, the nexus between the two. This journey requires a great deal of love, courage, faith, and hope. It's a journey that will at times be difficult because it will challenge our perception of what it means to be a "good" person. As with all enterprises of the Spirit, however, we will inevitably see a wider horizon of possibilities.

We are all spiritual mountain climbers, joined together with the bonds of the Spirit, called by God ever upward on our pilgrimage. Either all of us make it, or none of us do.

For reflection and discussion

Read once again the Scripture passage at the beginning of this chapter. Then, read the following passage from the conclusion of *The Scarlet Letter* by Nathaniel Hawthorne.

> But there was a more real life for Hester Prynne here, in New England, than in that unknown region where

> Pearl had found a home. Here had been her sin; here, her sorrow; and here was yet to be her penitence. She had returned, therefore, and resumed,—of her own free will, for not the sternest magistrate of that iron period would have imposed it,—resumed the symbol of which we have related so dark a tale. Never afterwards did it quit her bosom. But...the scarlet letter ceased to be a stigma which attracted the world's scorn and bitterness, and became a type of something to be sorrowed over, and looked upon with awe, and yet with reverence, too.

1. What are some parallels you see between the plight of the woman caught in adultery and the plight of Hester Prynne? What do you imagine Jesus would have had to say to Hester?

2. After reading the conclusion of *The Scarlet Letter,* imagine a conclusion for the story of the woman caught in adultery. How would she have been changed by this encounter with Jesus? What would her relationship be with those in the town who had condemned her?

3. How would you describe the encounter with grace experienced by the woman who is forgiven by Jesus?

4. In what ways were the two women ostracized from their communities. Does it seem fair? Why or why not?

CHAPTER 2

Conscience Formation and Social Justice

Among the messianic prophecies in the book of Isaiah is one sometimes referred to as the vision of the "peaceable kingdom." Using metaphorical language drawn from the natural world, the prophecy describes the effects of the coming of the Messiah who will set things right in the world as relationships, even between mortal enemies, are reordered:

> "The wolf shall live with the lamb,
> the leopard shall lie down with the kid,
> the calf and the lion and the fatling together,
> and a little child shall lead them."
>
> » **Isaiah 11:6**

This wondrous vision of Creation being restored to its initial innocence and goodness (symbolized by the child) promises a fulfillment of the Covenant promise brought into being from a Christian point of view through the life, death, and resurrection of Jesus. Isaiah's glorious vision celebrates a world in which right relationship has been restored. It is the hope contained in the Hebrew word for peace—*shalom*—which is much more than a greeting or a wish for a trouble-free day. It expresses the hopes and prayers of several millennia of the descendants of Abraham and Sarah, those related by blood and those related by Spirit, for a world purified of sin and its effects. Through the risen Christ, we can become co-creators of this new and also most ancient world intended by the Father before the beginning of time by applying ever more faithfully the social justice principles of the Church to our society. It is a very concrete way we can become the leaven Jesus speaks about to his disciples that gradually transforms the loaf that is society.

FINDING TRUE NORTH

Yet the complexity of the modern world, the law of unintended consequences (sometimes the plans intended to improve the quality of life can have unforeseen negative consequences), and the effects of original sin can blind us to what is truly good. How can we possibly know we are applying the social justice principles of the Church, or any of Jesus' teachings, in ways that will really serve the common good—that which is best for the greatest number of people without compromising the basic rights of anyone?

The morality of the Bible is rooted in an understanding of the nature of the universe known in Western philosophy as natural law theory. We believe that we live in a moral universe, that certain things are always inherently good, or inherently bad, because they are rooted in, or opposed to, the essential nature of God's love. We discover these inherent moral laws through conscience—described in the documents of the Second Vatican Council as a "law inscribed by God" in the human heart, a person's "most secret core and sanctuary." Within the bounds of our consciences, we are "alone with God, whose voice echoes in the depths" of our being.

Conscience is our most intimate point of contact with the Holy Spirit. A key duty of the magisterium (the teaching authority of the Church exercised by the pope and all of the bishops in communion with him) is to help us properly form our consciences—though never to replace them, as Pope Francis has written. That "secret core and sanctuary" within us where we are touched by the Spirit is alive and organic. It is very different from the superego, a term coined by pioneer psychologist Sigmund Freud, which refers to that voice of authority in our heads.

The superego includes all of the messages that we have received from our parents, our teachers, and the other authority figures in our lives. The superego is not alive, however. According to Freud, it forms when we are children, fossilizes, and remains with us in its juvenile form throughout our lives. The superego is incapable of integrating new information and experiences as we mature. If we use it as our moral guide, then we condemn ourselves to forever living with a child's perspective on the world. (It was the *faith* of a child, not the moral development of one, toward which Jesus exhorts us in the Scriptures.)

When the Council described conscience as our "sanctuary," the Council fathers had something very specific in mind. In an ancient temple, the sanctuary was the room within the structure where the god or goddess lived. This was holy ground. In the temple of Jerusalem, the sanctuary was known as the "Holy of Holies." In a Catholic church, this idea of "holy ground" is transferred to the tabernacle, that gold receptacle set off in a prominent place where the consecrated bread—the Body of Christ—is kept. To say that one's conscience is a sanctuary, therefore, is to say that this is the very place where God lives within each one of us. When we listen to the dictates of our conscience, we are listening to God. Whenever we are truly in touch with the Spirit at the core of our being, we can never be led astray.

LIFE IN THE FISHBOWL

During the five years I have commuted into Manhattan since starting my current teaching job, I have watched each day as what was an enormous hole in the ground became a gleaming high-rise residential tower. If we all possessed properly formed consciences, we would discern the movement of the Spirit in our daily lives clearly and powerfully. Applying the social justice principles of the Church in building a more just society would be as clear to us as the task facing the architects and construction workers involved in building that high rise. The lasting effect of original sin, however, is that no one's conscience has this kind of clarity. Not one of us is able to hear perfectly that voice of the Spirit within.

And even when we do sense the movement of the Spirit in our hearts, that doesn't guarantee we will choose to follow it. Once again, St. Paul: "For what I do is not the good I want to do; no, the evil I do not want to do—this I keep on doing" (Romans 7:19). Many times, our consciences are deformed by culpable or vincible ignorance. These terms refer to the damage that occurs to one's conscience because of the personal sins he/she commits. Like a rubber band that keeps getting stretched, our consciences get deformed more and more each time we do that which we know to be against the will of God. If a sin becomes habitual, the rubber band can break, and we can actually lose our ability to recognize that we are sinning.

When we bring social sin into the equation, things become even murkier. Invincible ignorance or erroneous conscience occurs when we fail to notice the injustice around us because we have come to accept social sin as the norm or, even more diabolically, as the will of God. Like fish in an aquarium, we are immersed in the "water" that consists of the various values, beliefs, and prejudices of our culture. And that water is cloudy.

A clear example of a devastatingly large blind spot in the history of America is racism. Look at any set of statistics—economic status, high school dropout rates, health statistics, prison populations—and you will see a sharp difference between the plight of many black Americans and the privileges of many white Americans. Though it is painfully and absolutely clear that the legacy of racism, sometimes described as America's original sin, continues to wreak havoc, to suggest to many white Americans that their attitude toward their black sisters and brothers may be tinged by the effects of racism is to invite, at best, a chilly reception.

Here again is that vicious cycle at work. The personal sins we commit make it harder for us to recognize, amid the complexity and the busyness of daily life, what is good and what is evil. This moral laxity allows social sin to infest and grow almost unnoticed. And as social sin and the subsequent injustice increases, our consciences become even more deformed. Injustice breeds more injustice. A person forced to live in abject poverty is constantly receiving the message that life is not particularly sacred. As a result, he/she will likely increasingly have a hard time seeing that sacredness in others. For those who do not suffer directly the effects of social injustice, ever increasing inequality is viewed by the more compassionate as a sad but unavoidable malady and the incentive to work for change gradually but certainly begins to erode. Jesus blesses those who "hunger and thirst" for justice, not those who passively wish for it.

SOCIAL JUSTICE AND PROPER CONSCIENCE FORMATION

When Pinocchio, the wooden puppet made by Papa Geppetto, gets his wish to become a real boy, he soon finds out this is harder than it looks. A puppet is controlled by strings and does not have to worry about making its own decisions. A real boy (or girl), on the other hand, does. If we could amend the advice of Pinocchio's friend, Jiminy Cricket, just a bit, we might say: "Always let your *properly formed conscience* be your guide." Perhaps we can't get out of the fishbowl we are in, but we can certainly see what is in the water more clearly. We have two sacred responsibilities—to form our consciences properly and to follow their dictates.

There are a number of factors that go into the care and feeding of a properly formed conscience. First and foremost comes prayer. If it is within our consciences that we hear God's "voice" most clearly, then it makes sense that the more practice we have in listening to God in prayer, the easier it will be to recognize the promptings of the Holy Spirit. The second primary means of proper conscience formation is the teaching of the Church. When the pope and the bishops apply the teachings of Jesus to the moral issues of our day, they are exercising their role as the magisterium of the Church. We believe that when our shepherds are acting in this role, they speak on Jesus' behalf, and they call on the faithful to submit to these teachings with the "assent of faith." To follow the teachings of the pope and the bishops with the assent of faith is to recognize that these teachings are guided by the same Holy Spirit who guides us toward the good in the sanctity of our consciences.

Increasingly, the magisterium of the Church is making use of the social justice principles to aid us in seeing the water in the fishbowl more clearly. It has become the practice of the United States bishops, for example, to offer the social justice principles of the Church as a guide for Catholic voters to use when selecting a candidate for president. The magisterium does not seek to promote any particular party or candidate; that would be a violation of the First Amendment and a serious abuse of this teaching authority. Rather, our leaders exhort us to evaluate a candidate's ability to support and uphold the common good based on these principles. Gradually, the blueprints for the City of God begin to take form and we can get to work.

As both individually and collectively we take up our respective crosses and begin the hard work of building a just society, we practice the third means of proper conscience formation. All of us are creatures of habit; *anything* we do repeatedly becomes easier to do as time passes. Eventually, some choices become second nature and we do them without really thinking. The good news is that habit doesn't just work against us; it can also work for us. While it is true, for example, that the more I lie, the easier it becomes to lie, it is also true that the more I practice the habit of telling the truth, the easier it becomes to be honest. The more I choose to be generous with my time, talent, and treasure, the more generosity becomes a way of life.

By cooperating with the Spirit in reforming and building up our consciences, we become more aware of both the personal sins we commit and the social sins to which we acquiesce. Gradually, we come to understand what it means to be truly free. Freedom, as Paul explains, is not the freedom to do whatever *we* want. It is the freedom to do whatever *God* wants. As the water in the fishbowl clears, the vicious cycle begins to reverse. The more faithfully we follow the teachings of Jesus, the harder it is to tolerate that which we know is harmful to ourselves and others. The Church provides us with the blueprints for the City of God. The Spirit, moving deep within our hearts, provides the grace and the motivation. The person with a properly formed conscience is able to see the world as Jesus sees it and to live as if the City of God in all its fullness were a reality now.

Not a bad definition of holiness.

For reflection and discussion

"The eye is the lamp of the body. So, if your eye is healthy, your whole body will be full of light; but if your eye is unhealthy, your whole body will be full of darkness. If then the light in you is darkness, how great is the darkness!" » **Matthew 6:22–23**

"Well, I can tell you it made me all over trembly and feverish, too, to hear him, because I begun to get it through my head that he *was* most free—and who was to blame for it? Why, *me*. I couldn't get that out of my conscience, no how nor no way. It got to troubling me so I couldn't rest; I couldn't stay still in one place. It hadn't ever come home to me before, what this thing was that I was doing. But now it did; and it stayed with me, and scorched me more and more. I tried to make out to myself that I warn't to blame, because I didn't run Jim off from his rightful owner; but it warn't no use, conscience up and says, every time, 'But you knowed he was running for his freedom, and you could a paddled ashore and told somebody.' That was so—I couldn't get around that noway. That was where it pinched."

» **Mark Twain, *Huckleberry Finn*, chapter 16**

1. In different ways, each quote above reveals something about the danger of a poorly formed conscience. In your own words, how would you state the danger?

2. Describe the darkness that ensues when the conscience, using Jesus' metaphor, loses its ability to "see."

3. In Mark Twain's classic passage, Huck Finn's moral struggle is the exact opposite of what it should be. He sees his willingness to help his friend Jim escape slavery as akin to stealing. What social sin accounts for the corruption of Huck's conscience? What does Huck's struggle suggest about the movement of grace in his life?

4. What are some other of the particular "darknesses" or moral blind spots of our culture? To what extent have they infected you? How do you know? (Keep the list you come up with to refer to as you read part 2 of this book.)

5. How do you go about making moral decisions? Who/What helps you do this? Who/What seems to get in the way?

CHAPTER 3

"NEW THINGS"

Rerum Novarum and the Birth of Modern Catholic Social Justice Teaching

"Love your neighbor as you love yourself." If you asked most people, Christian and otherwise, for a list of Jesus' five most important teachings, this would undoubtedly make the list. It is such an elegant and simple formula, one that exists in some form or another in every religion and culture. (My personal favorite comes from an African proverb: "Before you poke the bird in the eye with a stick, do it to yourself first.") It reminds us of two important truths: (1) the importance of loving ourselves, which really is only possible as we begin to recognize within our hearts the unconditional love God has for us, and (2) our vital roles as the conduits of God's love toward others.

For all of the vast changes in society that have occurred since the time of Jesus—economic, political, cultural, and technological—that simple moral instruction remains a true north star to guide human behavior. What has changed significantly, however, is the size of the neighborhood. During the time that Jesus lived, most people made their livings as subsistence farmers. With few exceptions, the percentage of human beings who lived in cities was relatively small. For about eight thousand years before the time of Jesus and for most of the two millennia after him agrarian societies were the norm. This meant that social interactions were mostly personal and intimate. Many villages were little more than extended families, and while farmers did journey into town for supplies and to socialize, for the most part everyone had at least a nodding acquaintance with everyone else. Occasionally, a stranger might pass through town, and the Bible is clear on the importance of showing hospitality, but this was the exception.

Then, beginning in the eighteenth century in Europe and gaining steam (pun intended) in the nineteenth century in America, a cataclysmic shift occurred. Cities expanded exponentially as the industrial revolution transformed society and more and more jobs shifted from the farm to the factory. In the United States, about 25 percent of Americans lived in urban areas in 1870. By 1916, that number had reached 50 percent (source: TheUSAonline.com). The shift from farming to factories is the second major social reorganization in human history. The first was the shift from hunter-gathers to farmers somewhere around ten thousand years ago.

When human beings moved from farms to cities and factories, society became more complicated. For starters, while even the poorest subsistence farmer could grow enough food to feed his family (though famines were not uncommon), factory workers were dependent on the wages they received to provide the necessities of life for their families. The merchants who supplied the essentials of food and clothing and household goods relied on the purchases made by these workers to support their own livelihood. And this was only the beginning. As the world has become more and more a vastly interconnected global village through the technology developed in the twentieth and twenty-first centuries (things like cars, airplanes, computers, and the internet), our way of life has become so much more complex.

DEHUMANIZATION

Not only is our global neighborhood much bigger than anything Jesus in his human nature could have imagined, but the vast majority of our interactions in this global village take place not in person but remotely (we almost never meet the workers who create the products we buy) and through cyberspace. It is a curious but consistently true aspect of human nature that our ability to treat our neighbor with love and respect is fundamentally influenced by whether or not we have a personal connection with him or her. Once we lose that connection, things take a turn for the worst in a hurry. The misery of the homeless or the incarcerated, of the malnourished or the refugees throughout the world might, on a day when we are not too distracted by the demands of our own lives, evoke our sympathy and even our prayerful attention. It is much less often, however, that this awareness motivates us to action and more infrequent that social change occurs. We are just too far removed from our sisters and brothers in crisis. More nefariously, our primitive tribal instincts increase their hold on us to the extent our sense of community decreases.

A PROPHETIC DOCUMENT

With a divinely inspired sense of what was happening and the implications for Christian discipleship from this industrial transformation, Pope Leo XIII wrote *Rerum Novarum* ("new things") in 1891. The new things Pope Leo wanted to call to the attention of all Catholics and all human beings of good will were the challenges threatening the neighborhood of humanity rooted in the rapidly changing social patterns. The fallout had become clear:

> In any case we clearly see, and on this there is general agreement, that some opportune remedy must be found quickly for the misery and wretchedness pressing so unjustly on the majority of the working class:... by degrees it has come to pass that working men have been surrendered, isolated and helpless, to the hard-heartedness of employers and the greed of unchecked competition....To this must be added that the hiring of labor and the conduct of trade are concentrated in the hands of comparatively few; so that a small number of very rich men have been able to lay upon the teeming masses of the laboring poor a yoke little better than that of slavery itself. » ***Rerum Novarum* 3**

Why was it that the so-called robber barons—men such as John D. Rockefeller or Andrew Carnegie or Cornelius Vanderbilt—caused so much misery for so many thousands as they reaped enormous profits for themselves and their families? Were they more evil than other men? That doesn't seem to ring true, given their devotion to their own families and their generous contributions to a variety of foundations and charities later in life. How, then, had they become deaf to the cry of the poor? What Pope Leo XIII recognized is the central theme of the first part of this book: as the human neighborhood grows in size and complexity, as we become more and more removed from the plight of others, our human capacity for compassion diminishes.

To "hunger and thirst" for justice as Jesus exhorts us to do is to make a conscious decision to see the world around us through the eyes of Jesus, to listen and respond to the needs around us with the heart of Jesus, and to allow the Spirit to guide us into the ways we can become the hands of Jesus. Doing all of this—an enterprise that is impossible without a deep personal and communal life of prayer—is to practice the virtue of social justice, a virtue that incorporates all of the social justice principles of the Church. According to Fr. John Hardon, this virtue "inclines one to co-operate with others in order to help make the institutions of society better serve the common good." It's a virtue that has to be cultivated.

Pope Leo XIII's encyclical reaffirmed and gave new life to the social justice teaching of the Church. Only the emphasis was new, however; the essential moral teachings found in the encyclical are those of the prophets of the Old Testament and of Jesus himself. At one point, Pope Leo quotes St. Thomas, the preeminent theologian and teacher of the Middle Ages:

> Man should not consider his material possessions as his own, but as common to all, so as to share them without hesitation when others are in need....True, no

> one is commanded to distribute to others that which is required for his own needs and those of his household....But, when what necessity demands has been supplied, and one's standing fairly taken thought for, it becomes a duty to give to the indigent out of what remains over. » ***Rerum Novarum* 22**

Pope Leo addresses both parts of the vicious cycle inherent in the relationship of personal and social sin. The pope first sounds the alarm about the overwhelming social injustice in modern society in which a very few are reaping enormous financial rewards from the labor of the many. Yet by referencing the teaching of St. Thomas, the pope also makes it clear that social sin did not just come upon us out of a clear blue sky; it is the human desire to hoard more than we need that provides the fuel for this fire.

Here is the key point, however: the human capacity for greed remains, presumably, as it always has been. The level of damage, however, that this particular aspect of original sin can wreak in industrial and postindustrial (technologically based) societies, versus agrarian ones, is much different. While the same sin motivated the wealthy man to take the poor man's only ewe lamb in the parable that the prophet Nathan told to King David (2 Samuel 12:1–12) and the "robber barons" of the nineteenth and early twentieth centuries, the "ewe lambs" they stole in the form of inadequate wages and poor working conditions numbered in the millions. And while King David was familiar enough with the situation of even the poorest farmers of his land to be able to recognize the sin (although not at first that the story was about him), the damage inflicted by greed and the other deadly sins today is often far removed from our daily experience. The cries of the poor are so distant that the natural connection to human empathy is broken. What is needed is a supernatural connection that, in the form of grace, builds upon our limited natural capacity for compassion and expands it so that it is large enough to take in the whole global village.

A LIVING LEGACY

Throughout the twentieth century, succeeding popes both reaffirmed and developed the social justice teaching of the Church first proclaimed by Pope Leo XIII. In his letter commemorating the one-hundredth anniversary of *Rerum Novarum*, Pope St. John Paul II went so far as to write that any attempt to proclaim the gospel in the modern world would fail if that proclamation did not include the social justice teaching of the Church:

> The "new evangelization," which the modern world urgently needs...must include among its essential elements a proclamation of the Church's social doctrine. As in the days of Pope Leo XIII, this doctrine is still suitable for indicating the right way to respond to the great challenges of today, when ideologies are being increasingly discredited. » ***Centesimus Annus* 5**

Reflecting the growing complexity and size of the neighborhood since the time of Pope Leo, particularly its global dimensions, Pope John Paul goes on to introduce a troubling new development. Not only are so many deprived of the basic necessities of life, but growing pockets of extreme poverty throughout the world have become so deep that there is simply no way out. It is a phenomenon the pope refers to as marginalization. The only way to overcome this evil, the pope continues, is "programed and responsible efforts on the part of the entire international community" (*Centesimus Annus* 35). Such a coordinated response is simply not possible without a widespread recognition of social sin and our collective responsibility for its existence.

In his encyclical *Caritas in Veritate*, Pope Benedict points out that social sin is a manifestation of original sin: "The Church's wisdom has always pointed to the presence of original sin in social conditions and in the structure of society" (34). Pope Francis writes and speaks about the diabolical fruit of marginalization: radical indifference. "To sustain a lifestyle which excludes others, or to sustain enthusiasm for that selfish ideal, a globalization of indifference has developed. Almost without being aware of it, we end up being incapable of feeling compassion at the outcry of the poor, weeping for other people's pain, and feeling a need to help them, as though all this were someone else's responsibility and not our own. *The culture of prosperity deadens us*" (*Evangelii Gaudium* 54, emphasis added). In these few words, our current pope captures the essential loss of empathy that has both contributed to and is fed by the yawning chasm between our limited ability to love our neighbor and the expanding size of the neighborhood.

There is much more to explore in the Church's teachings about social justice. A complete list of the social justice encyclicals can be found in the appendix of this book. Taken as a whole, this rich tradition reminds us that love of neighbor involves both charity and justice. Charity refers to the personal acts of kindness and generosity we do for others. Justice refers to the determination we make to work with others to build a more just society and, in the meantime, to limit our collusion with social sin. Jesus' act of charity in forgiving the woman caught in adultery is powerful indeed. Yet something essential would have been lost had he not first called out the social sin that overshadowed and contributed to the personal sin of the woman. So too the transformational power inherent within all of our personal acts of charity is diminished if we do not recognize an equally imperative responsibility toward the global neighborhood in all of its complexity.

For reflection and discussion

Is not this the fast that I choose:
to loose the bonds of injustice,
to undo the thongs of the yoke,
to let the oppressed go free,
and to break every yoke?
Is it not to share your bread with the hungry,
and bring the homeless poor into your house;
when you see the naked, to cover them,
and not to hide yourself from your own kin?
Then your light shall break forth like the dawn,
and your healing shall spring up quickly;
your vindicator shall go before you,
the glory of the LORD shall be your rear guard.

» **ISAIAH 58:6–8**

> It was a town of machinery and tall chimneys, out of which interminable serpents of smoke trailed themselves for ever and ever, and never got uncoiled. It had a black canal in it, and a river that ran purple with ill-smelling dye, and vast piles of building full of windows where there was a rattling and a trembling all day long, and where the piston of the steam engine worked monotonously up and down like the head of an elephant in a state of melancholy madness. It contained several large streets all very like one another, and many small streets still more like one another, inhabited by people equally like one another, who all went in and out at the same hours, with the same sound upon the same pavements, to do the same work, and to whom every day was the same as yesterday and to-morrow, and every year the counterpart of the last and the next. » ***HARD TIMES*** **BY CHARLES DICKENS, AS QUOTED ON WWW.VICTORIANWEB.ORG**

1. What insight into authentic Christian discipleship does Isaiah offer? What's the fundamental problem with a religion that lacks a commitment to social justice?

2. Update Isaiah's vision of social justice. What bonds do we need to break? What forms of oppression are particularly violent in our times? What yokes need to be broken?

3. Compare and contrast the ways that Pope Leo XIII and Charles Dickens, a near contemporary, capture the suffering wrought by the industrial revolution. What are the common experiences both emphasize?

4. How have things improved since the time of Charles Dickens in our society? What hasn't changed? What has become worse?

5. Imagine the prophet Isaiah, Pope Leo XIII, and Charles Dickens in conversation. What might that be like? What similarities and differences between the agrarian society of Isaiah and the industrial society of Pope Leo and Charles Dickens might they talk about? What might they agree upon as the essential change in attitude/action we need to make?

PART II

Reimagining the Seven Deadly Sins

CHAPTER 4

The Seven Deadly Sins

An Overview

Concupiscence. Webster's dictionary defines it as a "strong desire," especially in connection with sexual desires. Catholic moral teaching understands it as the human tendency toward sin, a desire to "worship the created instead of the creator." It is the lingering effect of original sin in human life. Original sin is the desperate human attempt to fill the yawning emptiness within—a response to, as Fr. Thomas Keating wrote, "the illusion that we are alone and unloved in an indifferent universe"—by demanding more from created goods than they can supply. The seven deadly sins provide a more comprehensive means to understand the nature of concupiscence. Each one of the sins—pride, greed, lust, wrath, envy, gluttony, and sloth—identify a fundamental pull away from God within the human heart.

GNOSTICISM

At first glance it might appear that the seven deadly sins, in fact the whole Christian understanding of concupiscence, is an insidious attempt on the part of religious folk to drive a wedge between the spirit and the body. Many hold the mistaken idea that one must choose between happiness in this life and misery in the next, or misery in this life and happiness in the next. Isn't that what St. Paul means, after all, when he makes a distinction between those born of flesh and those born of the spirit? (See Galatians 5:16–25 for an example.)

Such a concept directly contradicts the core Christian belief in the Incarnation. Our belief that the Son, second person of the Holy Trinity, took on human flesh in the person of Jesus of Nazareth signifies among other things the fundamental union of matter and spirit. The complete, eternal, and uncompromised union of Jesus' divine and human natures—known as the hypostatic union in Christian theology—was developed in great detail in the early Church in response to Gnosticism, one of the earliest Christian heresies. Rooted in the sharp distinction between body and soul that was a central part of ancient Greek philosophy, Gnosticism encompassed a collection of beliefs that either denied Jesus' human nature or understood that it had been totally absorbed by his divine nature. The dogma of the Incarnation, on the other hand, proclaims that flesh, and all of creation, is fundamentally holy and good.

THE COMMON DENOMINATOR

What, then, makes the seven deadly sins so deadly? Keep in mind the essence of original sin as worshiping the created rather than the Creator. Each of the deadly sins involves an excessive attachment to something in creation that is good in itself. It is the misuse of the created good that leads to sin. Take, for example, the sin of pride—better understood as arrogance. To take pride in one's self, to give glory to God for the ways in which we have, in cooperation with the Spirit, developed our gifts and shared them, to recognize that each of us has been created and are sustained in love—all of this is holy and good. Jesus teaches that you cannot love your neighbor—whether next door or around the world—unless you love yourself.

But what if I forget that God loves every other daughter and son God has created as much as God loves me? What if I begin to believe in my heart—which will inevitably show through in my actions—that I am more valuable than others? That my needs are more important? What if I begin to mistake my ego—the image I have of myself—for who I truly am in God's eyes? All of these subtle shifts in perspective move us from a healthy love of self to an excessive attachment to ourselves. This radical self-centeredness is the *sin* of pride. God is no longer the center of my life; I am. Good and evil, therefore, are no longer about what pleases or displeases God. They are now about what pleases or displeases *me*.

The same distortion caused by excessive attachment to what is otherwise good can be seen in the other deadly sins as well. (Keep in mind that the sin of pride acts as an accelerant for all of the rest, because the more I substitute my will for the will of God, the easier it becomes to justify sinful action.) The first creation story demonstrates God's blessing on our sexuality when God exhorts the newly created woman and man to "be fertile and multiply." The Second Vatican Council recognized not only this procreative value of sexual intimacy in marriage but also a unitive value. When two people who love one another with a covenantal love have entered into a sacramental marriage and express this love physically in the sexual union, that intimacy is nurtured and made deeper. When we become so attached to the pleasurable feelings of the genital expressions of our sexuality, however, that we seek to divorce them from their proper connection to the procreative and unitive dimensions of sexual intimacy in relationship, we commit the sin of lust.

God offers abundant material blessings in the form of the natural resources of the earth so that all human beings might have what they need. There is nothing wrong with seeking to provide oneself and one's family with the necessary share of those resources. (In Catholic social justice teaching, this is known as the universal destination of created goods.) There is something very wrong, however, when we are not satisfied with that which we need for our sustenance and begin to hoard surpluses of wealth or essential goods such as food, water, clothing, and shelter so that others lack basic necessities. When we become excessively attached to created goods and begin to seek from them a level of security or physical satiation or happiness that they are unable to supply, we are committing the sins of greed and gluttony.

The same principle holds true for the deadly sins that are less tangible. Being angry is a normal human emotion, and sometimes the appropriate emotion in the face of personal or social injustice. Jesus demonstrates this when he cleanses the temple (see John 2:13–17). All emotions are transitory and will wane.

If I feel so aggrieved, however, by the actions of another person toward me or by the unfairness of life or by God, I may become so attached to my anger that I do not want to let it go. Instead of *being* angry I start to *live* angry, and what was a healthy emotion hardens into the sin of wrath. There is nothing wrong with being ambitious and in taking inspiration from the achievements of others to motivate myself to do better and to contribute more to the world. If I become so attached to the other person's successes, however, as to denigrate the blessings in my life, or if I begin to begrudge the other person his/her achievements, then I begin to feel the effects of the sin of envy.

At the other end of the spectrum from misplaced ambition lies the sin of sloth. The good to which we become excessively attached in this case is leisure time. Recall the ending of the first creation story in which God sets aside the seventh day to celebrate and appreciate all of the good things God's will has brought into being. And if God is not so busy to take time off to celebrate and appreciate life, could we possibly be? It is essential that we take time to celebrate God's gifts and love in personal and communal prayer and worship, to relax from the daily demands of work, to enjoy and appreciate the company of family and friends, to pursue wholesome leisure time activities that renew and replenish us. We know that Jesus recognizes the importance of this because of one charge frequently leveled against him: "This man eats and drinks with sinners." May the same charge be leveled against us!

Yet we must not forget that the gifts we have been given through God's grace must be developed and shared or they will atrophy. Jesus reminds us that, to be his disciple, each of us must pick up his/her cross each day and do the hard work that conversion and love demand so that we can build the City of God in the here and now. If I choose to disengage with the world and stick my head in the sand so that I don't have to see the injustice around me, or if I engage in leisure time activities that are not wholesome, or if I overindulge in those that are, then a pursuit of leisure becomes the sin of sloth.

THE NEW FRONTIER

In offering us a meaningful way to recognize the darker impulses of our human nature, the seven deadly sins provide Catholics with a useful aid to discerning and getting to the roots of sin. As mentioned previously, however, such reflections can leave us with the false impression that keeping one's own house in order is the *only* requirement on the road to salvation. As outlined in the first part of this book, the shift that has occurred in Catholic moral teaching over the last century or so increasingly emphasizes the reality of social sin, the injustice that stems from it, and our responsibility to bring our faith into the public square and work with others to find solutions. This paradigm shift does not deny the reality of personal sin or the need for personal repentance and conversion—a close look at the excessive attachments outlined above will show that they all have social implications. It does confirm, however, that focusing solely on personal morality is not sufficient. Cooperating with grace and making use of the sacraments to confront our personal darkness makes us freer to engage in the hard work of social justice but leaves us at the threshold of holy transformation. We need to follow the example of Jesus in the story of the woman caught in adultery. Recall that Jesus does not approve of the sin of adultery, but he does put it in perspective. The greater sin in the background of the story is the social sin involved in viewing women as property.

Matter and spirit are inextricably bound together. The kingdom of God is among us, and our communal work for social justice is inextricably bound up with the full realization of that kingdom and our participation in it. For us to be fully open to the Spirit and thus fully engaged in the hard work of building that City of God in the here and now, we must recognize that *these same excessive attachments that cause personal sin are also at the root of all of the human-made injustices in society.* As for those evils grounded in the unpredictability of life—storms, earthquakes, floods, for example—our excessive attachments at the societal level ensure that these evils will inflict the most damage on those least able to deal with them. The remaining three chapters of this book are an invitation to begin reimagining what the seven deadly sins look like when we shift from a personal to a social point of view.

For reflection and discussion

> When Jesus saw the crowds, he went up the mountain; and after he sat down, his disciples came to him. Then he began to speak, and taught them, saying:
>
> "Blessed are the poor in spirit, for theirs is the kingdom of heaven.

"Blessed are those who mourn, for they will be comforted.

"Blessed are the meek, for they will inherit the earth.

"Blessed are those who hunger and thirst for righteousness, for they will be filled.

"Blessed are the merciful, for they will receive mercy.

"Blessed are the pure in heart, for they will see God.

"Blessed are the peacemakers, for they will be called children of God.

"Blessed are those who are persecuted for righteousness' sake, for theirs is the kingdom of heaven.

"Blessed are you when people revile you and persecute you and utter all kinds of evil against you falsely on my account. Rejoice and be glad, for your reward is great in heaven, for in the same way they persecuted the prophets who were before you."

» **Matthew 5:1–12**

Whatever is opposed to life itself, such as any type of murder, genocide, abortion, euthanasia, or willful self-destruction, whatever violates the integrity of the human person such as mutilation, torments inflicted on the body or mind, attempts to coerce the will itself; whatever insults human dignity, such as subhuman living conditions, arbitrary imprisonment, deportation, slavery, prostitution, the selling of women and children; as well as disgraceful working conditions, where people are treated as mere instruments of gain rather than as free and responsible persons;

> all these things and others like them are infamies indeed. They poison human society, and they do more harm to those who practice them than to those who suffer from the injury. Moreover, they are a supreme dishonor to the Creator. » **Pope St. John Paul II, *The Gospel of Life* [*Evangelium Vitae*], 3**

1. Contrast the qualities of the kingdom person Jesus offers in the Beatitudes with the seven deadly sins. How might the beatitude values serve as an antidote? Be as specific as you can.

2. How do you in your own life emphasize the holy impulses outlined in the Beatitudes and minimize the darker impulses that lead to the deadly sins? Where do you find yourself struggling? Where have you seen a real transformation by the power of the Spirit?

3. As a Church, which Beatitudes do we seem to be living out most faithfully? How? What impact have we had on transforming society? Which of the seven deadly sins seem to have a stranglehold on us? What must be done to foster a communal repentance and conversion?

4. When you consider the elements outlined in the excerpt from *The Gospel of Life*, referred to in other places by Pope John Paul II as forming a "culture of death," what connections to the seven deadly sins can you make? What social transformation is needed to overcome this culture? Be as specific as you can.

CHAPTER 5

PRIDE AND LUST

It was the happiest moment of my adult political life. Barack Obama had just been elected as the first African American President of the United States. The newscast I was watching invited Congressman John Lewis from Georgia to offer his thoughts on the groundbreaking election. This was no ordinary "talking head" interview; John Lewis was one of the co-leaders of the march across the Edmund Pettus Bridge in Selma, Alabama, on March 7, 1965. The courage and determination of Lewis and his fellow marchers to witness peacefully even as they were set upon by Alabama state troopers in a melee that came to be known as "Bloody Sunday" was instrumental in the passing of the Voting Rights Act later in 1965. During the interview on this election night, Congressman Lewis was so overwhelmed by emotion that he could barely speak. I teared up, too, feeling very proud to be an American. Though the struggle to overcome America's "original sin" of racism has taken too long and is marked with so much suffering and violence, here was clear evidence of progress.

Or so I thought. About eight and a half years later, it seemed that every white supremacist in America—could there really be so many in 2017?—gathered together in a torchlight procession in Charlottesville, Virginia, in what they labeled as a "Unite the Right" rally. The joyful scene in Lincoln Park, Chicago, on the night that Barack Obama was elected president seemed to be brutally replaced by a sad, hate-fueled parade of neo-Nazis and their ilk spewing their propaganda without shame in a park in Charlottesville. That pride I felt after the election of President Obama became infused with a deep sense of shame as I heard President Trump respond to the rioting that ensued—resulting in the death of counter-protestor Heather Heyer—by reminding us that there were "good people on both sides." What had gone wrong over those eight and a half years?

A SHAMEFUL LEGACY

The answer seems rather obvious upon reflection. While real progress has been made, racism remains alive and well in America. It's more subtle now; legal segregation has largely been dismantled, but economic segregation persists. Consider just a few statistics. According to the Pew Research Center, in 2016 the median wealth of non-Hispanic white households was $171,000. That is ten times the wealth of black households ($17,000). In other words, "Black households currently have only 10 cents in wealth for every dollar held by white households." And saddest of all, that gap has continued to widen. Of course, economics is only the tip of the iceberg.

The willingness of white Americans to tolerate racial injustice against their black sisters and brothers has roots that go deep into the corruptive influence of slavery. The enslavement of one race to build the wealth of another was easily justified by the racist fiction that people from Africa were subhuman, or at least of lesser intelligence than the superior white race. Seduced by the enormous economic advantage that came from enslaving an entire race of people, Americans in both the South, who directly benefited from this prejudice, and the North, who indirectly benefited through the use of Northern ships in the infamous Triangle Trade, transformed this fiction into a racist economic engine.

Even the more enlightened who recognized the fiction for what it was still saw themselves as a sort of benevolent caretaker class whose divinely ordained job it was to raise up the poor African from the darkness of his or her tribal origins into the sunlight of the Christian faith—viewed through the prism of white privilege. While no sensible white person would consciously hold such views today, to allow such cultivation of erroneous conscience for so many generations cannot be undone easily. Here is the sin of pride writ large, in the arrogance of white Americans who cling to a false narrative of American history that persistently overemphasizes the contributions of white men and seriously downplays the contributions of all others—especially the labor and suffering of the black slave. This false narrative poisons our ability at every turn to see—through genuine Christian eyes—what needs to be done to drive a stake into the heart of racism.

When the signers of the Declaration of Independence proclaimed that "all men are created equal" they had white male property owners in mind. At the heart of American history ever since has been the struggle to expand the right to "life, liberty, and the pursuit of happiness" to more and more people while facing the headwind of a prideful insistence that white male rights and privileges ought not be compromised. It might be helpful, before we go any further, to make a distinction between prejudice and racism. Prejudice—literally to "pre-judge"—involves making negative assumptions about an entire group of people based on misinformed stereotypes. It is a function of ignorance. Racism, on the other hand, requires the power to enforce one's prejudices on the other group—the ability to pass and enforce the Jim Crow laws in the southern United States that prevented African American citizens from full participation in society. The latter is an example of racism in action.

WHITE PRIVILEGE

There's a wonderful essay titled "White Privilege: Unpacking the Invisible Knapsack" by Peggy McIntosh, which points out a plethora of implicit and explicit inequalities in American society that support the imagined superiority of white Americans. The author encourages the reader to be more conscious of these "white privileges" and to do some soul searching by asking this question: "On a daily basis, what do I have that I didn't earn?" Start with the privilege of living in a segregated neighborhood, for example. In his book *The Silent Majority: Suburban Politics in the Sunbelt South,* Matthew D. Lassiter notes that, as a result of the Civil Rights Act, which prohibited all forms of legal segregation, municipalities switched to another tactic: "The suburban politics of middle-class warfare charted a middle course between the open racism of the extreme right and the egalitarian agenda of the civil rights movement, based in an ethos of color-blind individualism that *accepted the principle of equal opportunity under the law but refused to countenance affirma-*

tive-action policies designed to overcome metropolitan structures of inequality" (my emphasis added).

SEXISM

While racism in America is the original sin of the dominant culture, white privilege is not generally shared evenly between women and men. The widespread sexism in American society has significantly tilted that playing field in favor of white men as well. According to the U.S. Department of Labor, in 2017 the average salary for a man and woman in equivalent jobs was $52,146 and $41,977, respectively. This was true at all educational levels; comparing women and men with high school diplomas, college degrees, and graduate degrees consistently point to about a 20 percent difference in pay. While the "glass ceiling" is beginning to show cracks, the vast majority of those in positions of power are still white men.

Sexism's link to the sin of lust on a societal level is more indirect. Women may not be considered as property as they were in Jesus' time, but, again, deformation of conscience dies hard. Certainly, the signs abound that women in our society are considered less than fully equal. The Women's Center of Marshall University describes "rape culture" as an "environment in which rape is prevalent and in which sexual violence against women is normalized and excused in the media and popular culture." How is the so-called rape culture formed? Through "the use of misogynistic language, the objectification of women's bodies, and the glamorization of sexual violence," all of which to greater or lesser degrees are hallmarks of sexism. Eventually, these manifestations of sexism create "a society that disregards women's rights and safety." If lust on a personal level is an excessive attachment to sexual pleasure without the need for intimate relationship, then rape culture is the same manifestation but on a societal level. The #MeToo movement is an attempt at empowering women to combat this rape culture and to name those who perpetrate it.

LUST'S MOST DESPERATE VICTIMS

Just how deep the evil and degradation can go when lust infests society is revealed when we consider the illegal sex trade. It is a global epidemic—the logical conclusion of a sin that objectifies the person whose body is needed to satisfy sexual pleasure. There are more slaves in the world today—somewhere between 27 and 29 million—than there were when President Lincoln signed the Emancipation Proclamation in 1863. The vast majority of them are child laborers and women caught up in the sex trade.

Women get sucked into this cesspool in a variety of ways. Sometimes hopeful immigrants answer an ad promising them a better life only to find when they arrive—without money or any means of contacting anyone at home—that they have placed themselves in the clutches of a pimp. Sometimes a young woman, estranged from her own family, begins a relationship with what seems to be the man of her dreams but who is in fact grooming her for a life of prostitution. In places where poverty is so desperate and impervious to improvement, a family might sell a daughter into the sex trade in order to gain the finances needed to feed the rest.

Just as it's easy to blame the neo-Nazi for the sin of racism, it's easy to blame the heartless pimp for the sex trade. Yet no one would sell their soul to participate in such a vile business were it not immensely profitable. And the reason the sex trade is immensely profitable is because of the abundance of wealthy men who are eager participants. Bangkok, Thailand, for example is a popular destination for those interested in "sex tourism." So, too, is the host city for the Super Bowl in the United States each year. (Should this make us reconsider our love affair with the Super Bowl?)

Of course, the vast majority of us will never find ourselves at a white supremacist rally or as patrons of the sex slave trade. As people of good will, we genuinely hope and pray for an end to these evils. We try our best to treat others we meet as we would want to be treated, no matter their race or gender and to insist to our children that they do the same. We acknowledge we have prejudicial and lustful thoughts, and we do our best through prayer and action to honestly confront them. Isn't this commitment to overcoming the personal effects of pride and lust sufficient?

Based on the persistence of the societal evils outlined above, clearly it isn't. Recognizing the prejudicial and lustful impulses within us is most definitely a good starting point. Yet in proclaiming that all human beings are created in "the image and likeness of God" the Bible reveals to us that neither racism nor sexism were woven into the fabric of God's creation. It is the decision of generations of human beings to award privileges to some but not others that allowed these social sins and the injustice they bring to infest society. Therefore, it can only be the collective decisions of generations of human beings working together that will remove them from that fabric. As Mother

Teresa once said, "God will not make us do good. We must choose to do good." That is true not only on the personal level but even more so on the level of society.

As I sit here in all my white privileged maleness completing the final sentences in this chapter, the stink of my own hypocrisy is strong. If you cast the charge against me that was hurled at Jesus (though without the same justification), "Physician, heal thyself," you would be absolutely right to do so. Please don't allow the messenger to obscure the truth of the message. Jesus says that "to whom much is given much will be expected." If, like me, you have been the beneficiary of privileges you did not earn by virtue of your race and sex, how can you begin to pray for the wisdom and the courage and the conviction you need to work to diminish the imbalance if you cannot even bring yourself to recognize that such an imbalance exists? Let us pray for each other that the Spirit might open our hearts and minds to the truth.

For reflection and discussion

> Mary said to the angel, "How can this be, since I am a virgin?" The angel said to her, "The Holy Spirit will come upon you, and the power of the Most High will overshadow you; therefore the child to be born will be holy; he will be called Son of God. And now, your relative Elizabeth in her old age has also conceived a son; and this is the sixth month for her who

was said to be barren. For nothing will be impossible with God." Then Mary said, "Here am I, the servant of the Lord; let it be with me according to your word."
» **Luke 1:26–38**

Well, children, where there is so much racket there must be something out of kilter. I think that 'twixt the negroes of the South and the women at the North, all talking about rights, the white men will be in a fix pretty soon. But what's all this here talking about?

That man over there says that women need to be helped into carriages, and lifted over ditches, and to have the best place everywhere. Nobody ever helps me into carriages, or over mud-puddles, or gives me any best place! And ain't I a woman?...I could work as much and eat as much as a man—when I could get it—and bear the lash as well! And ain't I a woman? I have borne thirteen children, and seen most all sold off to slavery, and when I cried out with my mother's grief, none but Jesus heard me! And ain't I a woman?

...If my cup won't hold but a pint, and yours holds a quart, wouldn't you be mean not to let me have my little half measure full?

Then that little man in black there, he says women can't have as much rights as men, 'cause Christ wasn't a woman! Where did your Christ come from? Where did your Christ come from? From God and a woman! Man had nothing to do with Him.

If the first woman God ever made was strong enough to turn the world upside down all alone,

> these women together ought to be able to turn it back, and get it right side up again! And now they is asking to do it, the men better let them.
>
> » "AIN'T I A WOMAN" BY SOJOUNER TRUTH, 1851

1. Both passages above speak to the tremendous potential for transformation when we empower those disenfranchised by sexism and/or racism. How does each passage demonstrate the possibilities?

2. What does it say about God to recognize that God chose a powerless young woman to be at the center of salvation history? About the potential for good within the human heart? What other stories can you think of in which God works through the powerless and the marginalized?

3. Were Sojouner Truth alive today, what do you think she would say about the manner in which society has addressed racism and sexism in the last 150 years?

4. Consider Sojouner's response to "the little man in black." What is the truth Sojouner Truth sees in the story of the annunciation that is particularly relevant to women of her time and of all time? What are your feelings and thoughts?

5. "If my cup won't hold but a pint, and yours holds a quart, wouldn't you be mean not to let me have my little half measure full?" Explain what Sojouner Truth means. In what ways do we continue to hoard our quarts in relation to racism and sexism?

CHAPTER 6

GREED, GLUTTONY, AND SLOTH

> So God created humankind in his image, in the image of God he created them; male and female he created them. God blessed them, and God said to them, "Be fruitful and multiply, and fill the earth and subdue it; and have dominion over the fish of the sea and over the birds of the air and over every living thing that moves upon the earth."...God saw everything that he had made, and indeed, it was very good.
> » **GENESIS 1:27–31**

Sometimes in our rush to consider original sin we overlook the grace of original blessing. The story that invites us to ponder prayerfully and deeply over the mystery of sin is found in Genesis 3. Genesis 1 and 2, however, offer us two distinct and independent creation stories that, each in its own way, celebrate the sacramental quality of creation and the benevolent love of God. All creation is blessed because it comes from the mind of God—more accurately, from the heart of God, who is love. Human beings stand at the pinnacle of that creation, identified in Genesis 1 as having been created in the "image and likeness" of God. Not only were we brought into being through God's love; we have been created in such a way that we have the ability to do what no other creature or created thing can do—love God back. This is the reason that St. Thomas Aquinas refers to human beings as "the lowest form of spiritual life."

THE LOSS OF RIGHT RELATIONSHIP

If we were able to return God's love perfectly, the way that Jesus modeled for us, there would be no human being who lacked the essential resources needed to live a fully human life. According to our belief in the universal destination of created goods, the natural resources of creation are abundantly sufficient for this purpose. We would recognize the sacred character of creation as well as our fundamental relationship with all living things. Social injustice would not exist because we would not tolerate it; we would recognize our responsibilities to care for one another and would do whatever was necessary as a society—and make whatever personal sacrifices were necessary—to make things right again. The very thought of polluting our natural environment or using the earth's natural resources in an unsustainable way would be as abhorrent to each of us as doing violence to our own bodies. Alas, as Genesis 3 so profoundly reveals, that very thing that makes us like God—our ability to discern God's will and to choose whether or not to follow—can also be our undoing. God's will is that we live in right relationship with one another and with creation, but that can happen only when we are, first and foremost, in right relationship with God.

The deadly sins of greed, gluttony, and sloth share a common element that offers some insight into why we so often take actions individually and, much more destructively, as a society that mar the original blessing of God. Not one of us is immune to the incessant cry of our egos for *more*. More wealth, which we think will insulate us against all evil and which will increase our self-worth. Ever more resources, primarily in the form of consumer products, which we think will make us happier. And as it becomes uncomfortably clear that such efforts fail to address what is at the core of our insatiable wants, we begin to replace wholesome leisure activities with various means of escapism that simply numb us from the emptiness within. When Mary notes in the Magnificat that God "sends the rich away empty" she is not condemning the rich; rather, she is acknowledging that God can never satisfy those in the grip of the sins of greed and gluttony and sloth because their excessive attachments stoke desires that can never be fulfilled.

The social dimension and effects of these three sins is enormous. Just take a few moments to reflect on this one statistic and its implications: According to the Global Policy Forum, the richest one billion people in the world—that's less than 15 percent of the world's population—use 80 percent of the world's natural resources. How can the common good ever be served if 85 percent of the population has to make due with what's left? Our excessive attachment to wealth and our relentless consumption of the natural resources of the earth in the developed world have produced massive social inequality in a multiplicity of ways. We'll focus here briefly on two major ones: enormous economic inequality and the imminent and perhaps irreversible effect of climate change on ecosystems and human society.

THE RISING ECONOMIC INEQUALITY

The size and scope of economic injustice in the world—the manifestation of greed on a global scale—is impossible to ignore for anyone with ears to hear and hearts to care. We have already reflected on some examples from the social justice encyclicals of the Catholic Church; I would encourage you to explore them in greater detail. According to the World Bank (www.worldbank.org), almost half of the world's approximately 7.7 billion people live on less than $5.50 a day. The gap is not much smaller in the United States: according to Federal Reserve data as reported through the Rueters news service, the wealthiest 20 percent of Americans held 88 percent of the country's wealth in 2016. At the other end of the spectrum, the squeeze gets worse and worse: the number of Americans receiving food stamps is over thirty-nine million, a 40-percent growth in the last ten years. According to a StreetEasy poll from 2017, rents in New York City have risen twice as fast as wages over the past ten years, not coincidently occurring at the same time as a 70-percent increase in homeless people sleeping in the city's shelters (The Coalition for the Homeless).

It is important to remind ourselves regularly that there is nothing inevitable about any of this. The warping of the free market economy from what it is intended to be in theory—the most efficient way to allocate limited goods and services—is rooted in our excessive attachments. Pope St. John Paul II puts it this way: "It is not wrong to want to live better; what is wrong is a style of life which is presumed to be better when it is directed towards *'having' rather than 'being,'* and which wants to have more, not in order to be more but in order to spend life in enjoyment as an end in itself" (*Centessimus Annus* 35; my emphasis added). The only way to overcome those attachments at the heart of greed, gluttony, and sloth is to ask, reflect on, and act on the three questions, individually and in our policy making, that the U.S. bishops advise us to consider in their Economic Justice for All pastoral letter (1986): What does the economy do for people? What does it do to people? And how do people participate in it? These questions, when taken into prayer and serving as food for discussion among people of good will, might inspire a fourth: Can it possibly be God's will for an economic system to increasingly disenfranchise some while hardening the hearts of others?

WHAT IS DOMINION?

This insatiable desire to possess and to consume so deeply woven into our economic system doesn't stop with the accumulation of wealth and the purchase of consumer goods. It affects the very way we look at the natural world and our relationship with it. During the entirety of his pontificate thus far, and expressed most clearly in his encyclical *Laudato Si'* (On the Care and Concern for the Environment) Pope Francis is sounding a clarion call to reconsider what the Bible means when it says that God has given us "dominion" over the rest of creation. Our excessive attachments and desires, amplified by the technology of the industrial revolution, have caused us to replace dominion—the responsibility to be good stewards of the earth's resources—with domination, the idea, spawned of gluttony, that we have the right to treat the natural resources of the earth as the personal property of the rich. Under this mindset, which ignores any sense of original blessing, we have given ourselves permission to rape and pillage the land and the sea without any thought to long-term effects or how the degradation will particularly affect the poor. The CO2 that took millions of years to find its way into the ground and into the sea has been in large part thrown back into the atmosphere over the past 150 years. How could people who are in tune with the rhythms of nature think that such behavior would not have long-term implications? As the earth becomes hotter, sea level rises, and weather patterns continue to change. The effects of such devastation won't be felt equally by all, however; it is the poor who will suffer the most.

For the first time in the social justice teaching of the Church, Pope Francis makes explicit what was always implicit—environmental devastation is a manifestation of sin and is a major social justice issue. "The violence present in our hearts, wounded by sin, is also reflected in the symptoms of sickness evident in the soil, in the water, in the air, and in all forms of life. This is why the earth herself, burdened and laid waste, is among the most abandoned and maltreated of our poor....We have forgotten that...our very bodies are made up of her elements" (*Laudato Si'* 2). The pope continues: "Creation is 'harmed' where we ourselves have the final word, where everything is simply our property and we use it for ourselves alone" (6).

It is obvious that greed and gluttony play a major role in the way we are consuming the world's resources, poisoning the land and water with our refuse (scientists estimate that in the not-too-distant future the weight of plastic in our oceans will outweigh the total weight of fish), and raising the temperature of the earth at a much faster rate than natural causes would account for. Yet the pope reminds us that sloth should not be overlooked either. In the refusal of too many to acknowledge the overwhelming scientific evidence of human contributions to global warming, the pope sees something more than merely a lack of understanding: "Obstructionist attitudes, even on the part of believers, can range from denial of the problem to indifference, nonchalant resignation, or blind confidence in technical solutions" (14). Sloth is, at its core, a willful laziness, a determination not to know the truth because it might force one to make undesirable changes in her/his lifestyle.

Yet for all of its calls for change and clear attempts to shake us out of our complacency, *Laudato Si'* is, in essence, a proclamation of hope. As with lust, the key to changing attitudes and behaviors—in this case affecting the natural world—is to rediscover original blessing and replace the vision of creation as commodity with the original vision of creation as sacrament. In one of the most poetic verses in the encyclical, Pope Francis writes: "Every creature is the object of the Father's tenderness, who gives it its place in the world. Even the fleeting life of the least of beings is the object of his love, and in its few seconds of existence, God enfolds it with his affection" (77). He continues: "The natural environment is a collective good, the patrimony of all humanity and the responsibility of everyone. If we make something our own, it is only to administer it for the good of all. If we do not, we burden our consciences with the weight of having denied the existence of others" (95).

As is expressed throughout our social justice teaching since 1891, and the moral teachings of the Church since Jesus himself preached in the synagogues and the towns and the fields of Galilee, God's hope and promise for us is that we discover what it means to be truly free. This will require breaking our excessive attachments as individuals and as a society. Toward the end of the encyclical, Pope Francis makes this clear: "Our freedom fades when it is handed over to the blind fears of the unconscious, of immediate needs, of self-interest, and of violence" (105).

For reflection and discussion

O LORD, our Sovereign,
  how majestic is your name in all the earth!
  You have set your glory above the heavens.
Out of the mouths of babes and infants
  you have founded a bulwark because of your foes,
  to silence the enemy and the avenger.
When I look at your heavens, the work of your fingers,
  the moon and the stars that you have established;
what are human beings that you are mindful of them,
  mortals that you care for them?
Yet you have made them a little lower than God,
  and crowned them with glory and honor.
You have given them dominion over the works of your hands;
  you have put all things under their feet,
all sheep and oxen,
  and also the beasts of the field,

the birds of the air, and the fish of the sea,
whatever passes along the paths of the seas.
O Lord, our Sovereign,
how majestic is your name in all the earth!

» **Psalm 8:1–9**

Thousands of tired, nerve-shaken, over-civilized people are beginning to find out that going to the mountains is going home; that wildness is a necessity; and that mountain parks and reservations are useful not only as fountains of timber and irrigating rivers, but as fountains of life. Awakening from the stupefying effects of the vice of over-industry and the deadly apathy of luxury, they are trying as best they can to mix and enrich their own little ongoings with those of Nature, and to get rid of rust and disease.

» **John Muir, *Our National Parks***

1. Read Psalm 8 slowly and prayerfully. What images stand out for you? How does the psalm make you feel? How does it influence your perspective on the created world around you and your place in it?

2. In the context of this psalm, what do you think the psalmist meant by "dominion"? Why? How does this psalm develop the concept of original blessing?

3. Have you ever felt "nerve-shaken and overcivilized"? What do these terms mean to you?

4. Can you call to mind a time you have experienced the natural world as a "fountain of life"? (Take some time to reflect, describe, and write about the experience.) How often have you had these experiences?

5. What do you think are the "rust and diseases" of today that prevent us from seeing the majesty of God's creation? How about "the deadly apathy of luxury"?

CHAPTER 7

WRATH AND ENVY

> And as she walked away, I looked at my wife. And then and there I thanked the good Lord, for the gifts in my life....Some of God's greatest gifts are unanswered prayers. » GARTH BROOKS

In the song "Unanswered Prayers," Garth Brooks recalls a time when he and his wife ran into the girl he had a serious crush on in high school. In a flash of insight he realizes how God knew all along what was best for him and what a graced life he had been leading. This is the essence of original blessing on a personal level—to realize you have had everything you needed all along, sometimes (often?) in spite of yourself, and to become aware just how much our loving God has your back.

How easy it is, though, for any one of us to forget this. And as we begin to lose touch with the abundance of blessings that surrounds us, original sin—that illusion we are alone and unloved in an indifferent universe—gets hold of us with a vengeance. Why is life so unfair to us, we begin to wonder. What right does he/she have to that gift/person/thing? How dare he/she take what is rightfully mine? Why doesn't God ever listen to me? Gradually, almost imperceptibly, such resentments find a home in us and we cling to our anger and jealousy as if they were sacred possessions. We wrap these dark cancers in the finest cloth and hold them tight to our chests. Forgiveness and contentment become more like strangers than friends to us, and we mock them in others as our urge to curse overcomes our desire to bless. We find ourselves in the grips of the deadly sins of wrath and envy.

While all of the deadly sins have taken their toll on our society and, especially, on the most vulnerable within it, wrath and envy have grabbed our national soul in ways I haven't experienced at any other time in my adult life. Those a bit older than me who clearly remember the tumult of the Vietnam War era may disagree, but fifty years is still a long time. Certainly, there is an unholy connection between these two sins and the rest of the seven. When we are arrogant, for example, we take much more offense at perceived slights against ourselves and our views than is justified. More directly relevant to our current troubles, the greed and gluttony of large multinational companies who gobble up both human and natural resources for the sake of the rich have produced an awful legacy. As the gap between the rich and the poor grows, deep resentment simmers just below the surface among the increasing numbers of people who have been denied the benefits of globalization. The resulting wrath and envy harden the hearts of good people in their desperation, cloud their good judgment, and make them vulnerable to unscrupulous demagogues who, in order to satisfy their lustful desire for power, fire up the rage and bitterness. Those in the grip of wrath and envy are encouraged to look for scapegoats; and so the rich get richer while the marginalized tear one another apart.

Wrath in the public square on the parts of both progressives and conservatives has almost paralyzed us in our efforts to find common ground and work for the common good. When the two major political parties, fueled by irresponsible invective, begin to resemble warring tribes rather than two different approaches to addressing the nation's complex issues, nothing can really get solved. Rather than appreciate the freedoms and the good quality of life which, despite our troubles, can still be readily found in America, we envy those in past generations whom we think experienced a greatness that has now faded. We do not reckon with the power of nostalgia to blot out the pain, terror, and injustice of the past. On a personal level, these two deadly sins poison relationships and breed hostility. On a societal level, they become a powder keg that too often explodes into violence.

Nowhere is the destructive effect of wrath so clearly seen as in the epidemic of gun violence in America. According to the Brady Campaign to Prevent Gun Violence, more than 35,000 people in the United States die from gun violence each year. When we consider the plight of those who don't die, the number is much higher: 124,760 Americans are shot each year, of which over 10 percent (17,207) are children or teenagers. Between 2000 and 2017, there have been 250 FBI-designated "active shooter" incidents resulting in more deaths and injuries than have occurred in recent years on the battlefields where our troops are stationed.

Columbine. Virginia Tech. Sandy Hook. Charleston. Orlando. Las Vegas. Parkland.... We've almost reached the point where the mass shooting fails to register. Yet for all of their horror, these mass shootings that grab headlines pale in comparison to the regular gun violence on a nightly basis, often in poor communities, that accounts for many more deaths and injuries. Most disturbing of all are the staggering numbers of shooters who have a history of domestic violence and the 60 percent of gun deaths related to suicide. The widespread availability of guns is not making us safer. These tangible expressions of our collective wrath are mostly making sacrificial victims out of our most desperate and most vulnerable citizens.

The motivations of the shooters themselves are varied and mostly hard or impossible to understand. Misogyny and untreated mental illness certainly play a role. We would be naïve, however, if we ignored as a contributing cause the wrathful hate speech that can be found in too many places on the internet and which is often cited in notes left by the shooters. While the worst of that hate speech exists on the margins, at the center of our culture is a glorification of violence in many of the movies and television shows we watch. When you combine an individual who is psychologically disturbed, the implicit and explicit violent messages polluting the water of the fishbowl in which we all swim, and the widespread availability of guns in our society (according to the Brady Campaign there are more guns than people in the United States) the potential for catastrophe is always present. Add to that volatile mix overwhelming despair—which can be the result of wrath turned inward—and it may well seem to a deeply troubled soul that going out in a perceived blaze of glory is the best he/she can hope for from life. It continues to puzzle me why a Church that recognizes the sanctity of life from conception to natural death as the primary directive and that bears such unambiguous witness on behalf of unborn children is so comparatively silent when faced with the slaughter of born children who are the primary victims of the weaponization of wrath.

As wrath and envy increase, tolerance, generosity, and compassion inevitably decrease. What we are witnessing in the immigration crisis in America at this time is a perfect storm in which wrath and envy—and the feelings of outrage, deprivation, and denial that inevitable follow—are inflaming the historical schizophrenia of the American psyche. At times we glorify the immigrants who have built our country, and at other times we demonize them. On the one hand, we sing the praises of immigrants who have contributed to the quality of life in America and for all humanity in many fields—Albert Einstein, Elie Wiesel, Gloria Estefan, Yo Yo Ma, John Muir, just to name a few. On the other hand, our xenophobia is never far below the surface. Newly arrived immigrants in any age are often viewed with contempt if not outright suspicion. We carry around in our heads a picture of "true Americans"—which, unless we are thinking of Native Americans, is mostly nonsense—and use our prejudices as a mirror in which we can point out all that is lacking in those newly arrived. In times of heightened fear, as in the case of the Japanese Americans interred as a result of the bombing of Pearl Harbor, we act on those suspicions.

All of the above applies to those who have legally immigrated to the United States. What makes the "perfect storm" of our present crisis so much more dangerous is the enormous number of those emigrating into the United States across our southern border illegally. Certainly, a country has a right to defend its borders, and lawbreaking, generally speaking, should never be condoned. It is a gross violation of the common good to allow unrestricted immigration without any thought as to how society will provide for the immigrant and what the impact will be of large, unanticipated arrivals of immigrant populations into communities lacking the infrastructure to provide for the fundamental needs of all. Clearly, there is a need for Congress and the person occupying the presidency to work together to reach legal, reasonable, and compassionate solutions.

However, is the core of the outrage many feel toward the illegal immigrant at this time truly grounded in righteous anger that laws are being broken? Given the ways that wrath and envy are inflaming that streak of xenophobia in the national psyche, this is doutbtful. Too often the wave of undocumented immigrants is described as an "invasion force," a patently absurd phrase based not on any objective facts but as a rationalization for our fears. What we see in the heart of our current immigration crisis is the devastation the seven deadly sins have wrought on a hemispheric level. Perhaps nowhere else in the world is the economic devastation caused by arrogance, greed, and gluttony as obvious as in the yawning chasm in the standard of living between the United States and Canada and the Central American countries of Nicaragua, Guatemala, El Salvador, and Honduras. The vast majority of those attempting to enter the United States from the south are desperately searching for a better life for themselves and their families. What I often ask myself when I sense the rumblings of resentment and fear in my own heart is this: If I thought my children faced a future of either being forced to join a gang or be killed by a gang, what wouldn't I do to protect them? What wouldn't you do?

The inflamed xenophobia described above has global implications as well. Fueled by the fear and grief—the seedbed for wrath—generated from the attacks against the United States on September 11, 2001, our openness to accepting refugees from devastated areas of the world is closing. According to a CNN report, there was a 65-percent drop in admissions during 2017 when 33,400 people were resettled. According to the International Rescue Committee (IRC) things seemed to become worse again in 2018 when it appears that the United States resettled only 21,292 refugees. Overall the annual cap is down from 110,000 in 2016 to 45,000 at the time of this writing.

This is happening at a time when estimates by the United Nations suggest that the number of refugees in the world today (25.9 million) is higher than at any time since World War II. What makes the situation even more tragic is that half of these refugees are children. In a glaring example of the global indifference about which Pope Francis speaks, about a third of these refugees (6.7 million) are hosted by the world's poorest countries—societies least able to handle such massive migration.

Again, there is nothing wrong with a country seeking to set reasonable quotas for immigration and for accepting refugees. One of the most important roles a government serves is to protect the safety of its citizens; therefore, those arriving from countries in which terrorism thrives ought to receive careful scrutiny. Yet when the history of this era is written and we stand before Christ on that final day, responsible not just for our individual conduct but for what we did or didn't do to promote justice and compassion in our society, how will we be judged in response to, according to Jesus, the only criteria that will matter: "Whatever you do to the least of my sisters and brothers, you did to me"?

Overcoming the xenophobic waves that are currently washing over us is not a simple process. There are many real and imagined psychological, emotional, and historical factors at work. Using the lens of the seven deadly sins, however, can help us become more aware of one: envy. Thanks in large part to a consumer-based economy stoked by a constant barrage of advertisements, the general human tendency to always want more leads us to often focus our attention on the comings and goings of the rich. We want what they have. In our frenetic pursuit of the American dream, we feel we can get ahead only by leaving others behind, and we fear that the newly arrived immigrant or refugee may try to take what is (perceived to be) rightfully ours. Rather than opting for the generosity of the gospels toward the poor, we see them as a threat to our chances of achieving a better way of life. Were we, like the Garth Brooks song says, more appreciative of the blessings we do possess, we would be more willing to share those blessings with others.

Those who strongly feel we need to do a better job of controlling our borders and be more careful about who we allow into our country are not evil. Those who feel we must never let practical considerations get in the way of showing the compassion of Christ to the refugee and the immigrant, even if that means a certain level of risk and disorder, are not evil. Both have an important message; the concerns of both need to be held in dialogue so that, together as a country, we might create laws and policies that best serve the common good. As long as wrath and envy continue to be used as the building blocks of a cold, impenetrable wall around our national heart, however, such a consensus will never be reached. Caught up in a whirlwind of rage and deprivation, we lose touch with a fundamental truth of our faith—that those immigrants and refugees who seek our aid are a part of the neighborhood in which Christ commands us to love.

Best perhaps to let Pope Leo have the last word:

> The following duties bind the wealthy owner and the employer: not to look upon their work people as their bondsmen, but to respect in every man his dignity as a person ennobled by Christian character. They are reminded that, according to natural reason and Christian philosophy, working for gain is creditable, not shameful, to a man, since it enables him to earn an honorable livelihood; but to misuse men as though they were things in the pursuit of gain, or to value them solely for their physical powers—that is truly shameful and inhuman. Again, justice demands that, in dealing with the working man, religion and the good of his soul must be kept in mind.
>
> » ***Rerum Novarum* 20**

Replace the word "work people" and "working man" with "immigrant" and "refugee," and the quote's relevance becomes even more immediate.

For reflection and discussion

My heart was heavy, for its trust had been
Abused, its kindness answered with foul wrong;
So, turning gloomily from my fellow-men,
One summer Sabbath day I strolled among
The green mounds of the village burial-place;
Where, pondering how all human love and hate
Find one sad level; and how, soon or late,
Wronged and wrongdoer, each with meekened face,
And cold hands folded over a still heart,
Pass the green threshold of our common grave,
Whither all footsteps tend, whence none depart,
Awed for myself, and pitying my race,
Our common sorrow, like a mighty wave,
Swept all my pride away, and trembling I forgave!

Emily Dickinson, "Forgiveness"

But I say to you that listen, Love your enemies, do good to those who hate you, bless those who curse you, pray for those who abuse you. If anyone strikes you on the cheek, offer the other also; and from anyone who takes away your coat do not withhold even your shirt. Give to everyone who begs from you; and if anyone takes away your goods, do not ask for them again. Do to others as you would have them do to you.

> If you love those who love you, what credit is that to you? For even sinners love those who love them. If you do good to those who do good to you, what credit is that to you? For even sinners do the same. If you lend to those from whom you hope to receive, what credit is that to you? Even sinners lend to sinners, to receive as much again. But love your enemies, do good, and lend, expecting nothing in return. Your reward will be great, and you will be children of the Most High; for he is kind to the ungrateful and the wicked. Be merciful, just as your Father is merciful.
>
> Do not judge, and you will not be judged; do not condemn, and you will not be condemned. Forgive, and you will be forgiven; give, and it will be given to you. A good measure, pressed down, shaken together, running over, will be put into your lap; for the measure you give will be the measure you get back.
>
> » **Luke 6:27–38**

1. Reflect on the experience Emily Dickinson describes in the graveyard. Why was she able to let go of her wrath and forgive? What lessons can we take and apply to our lives?

2. What is the similar theme expressed both in the poem and in the teachings of Jesus? Why would recognizing these truths be an antidote to wrath and envy?

3. What does Jesus mean when he says, "The measure you give will be the measure you get back?"

4. Call to mind a person or a group with whom you feel you have nothing in common. Reflecting on the above readings, come up with some common ground. Does this exercise change, even in a small way, your attitudes or perspective? In what way?

5. What is the "sad level" of love and hate Emily Dickinson refers to? How does this view compare and contrast with the level of love that Jesus calls for in the passage from Luke's gospel?

CONCLUSION

Avoiding the Devil's "One-Two" Punch

This book is intended to be a leaven within the dough of the traditional Catholic mindset concerning the seven deadly sins. It never was true that faithful Catholicism rested primarily in a strict adherence to a personal moral code. St. Paul writes again and again about the futility of such an endeavor; all depends on the grace of Christ and the victory won through Jesus' life, death, and resurrection. Jesus always compels us to recognize the unconditional love of God within us and then, as we are being changed, to allow ourselves to be transformational instruments in the world. In the prophetic acts of Jesus' own ministry—his implicit challenge of the sexism of his day as outlined in chapter 1, his call for a radically new way of worship demonstrated in his cleansing of the temple, his subtle act of subterfuge when he called upon his followers to "give to Caesar what is Caesar's but to God what is God" (implying that there were indeed many things that do not belong to Caesar), all of this and more are Jesus' attempts to work for social justice in his own time and to change attitudes. From a historical point of view, one could make a good case that it was the reason he was crucified.

Such a commitment to social justice is all the more imperative in the world we live in today, where our interconnectedness grows in its complexity each day and the size of the neighborhood is ever more vast. There is no going back; it is simply impossible to love one's neighbor in the way that Jesus means without rejecting both personal sin, social sin, and the vicious cycle between the two. Today we are experiencing Moses' call to "choose life and not death" in a new way. We can find many examples of virtual communities that unite people all around the world in various good causes and spiritual practices, but we can also find too many examples of groups promoting hate speech on the web. Our capacity to bind together for the common good, aided by technology, is greater than it ever has been in all of human history, yet that same technology can be used to bring civilization to its knees. Will we adhere to Pope Francis' exhortation to "build bridges and not walls"? The choice, as it always has been, is up to us.

If all of this seems too daunting, if the amount of suffering in the world feels so enormous and so complex that it seems impossible to know where to start, keep in mind two important points. The first is about God, who loves us beyond our ability to imagine, who roots mightily for us to succeed, and who will do anything to help us except to compromise free will. We are in the hands of a God who not only loves us but believes in us. (Whatever the state of your belief in God at the moment, know that God's belief in you is rock solid.) Why else would God launch the enterprise of human redemption through a human woman and her divinely incarnated but fully human son? Why else would God have graced us with free will in the first place? And in addition to the waterfall of grace God constantly pours into our lives through the Spirit, we have quite an enormous rooting section among the saints in heaven—some canonized, most not—who pray for us and tap into, on our behalf, a vast treasury of grace all of the time.

The second point concerns the devil. Just as the devil is able to quote Scripture for his own purposes so he is able to twist this emerging global consciousness for his own ends. I think of this as the devil's one-two punch. Initially, evil thrives on selfishness. Thus the danger of the seven deadly sins, any one of which by fostering excessive attachment to a created good ultimately contributes to our separation from one another and from God. Yet grace is relentless and effective, and as we are gradually turned from self-centeredness toward other-centeredness (often with us kicking and screaming along the way!) the devil begins to change his tactics. Suddenly, the immensity of the brokenness and the suffering and the pain and the hopelessness of the world begins to overwhelm us. Our efforts to show compassion, like a light turned inward, appear only to show us how even our most sincere efforts to do good are tinged with sin, how often our best intended actions lead to unintended consequences. We want to shout out with St. Paul, "Oh what a wretched man (or woman) I am!"—or at least pull the covers over our heads and weep into our pillows. What we might think is humility is actually the sin of pride masquerading as something holy. Did we really think God expected us to save the world on our own?

The best word I've ever come across to describe this phenomenon is "splatterscreen." It's a term originally used to identify cheesy B horror movies that give the viewer an overabundance of bloodshed and gore. In the context of our modern media, the term has been applied to the internet's ability to bring an overabundance of bad news in graphically horrific detail to our attention much more quickly and consistently than ever before. It's easy to become overwhelmed and feel helpless.

We suffer burnout or overload; our hearts begin to harden not out of maliciousness but out of a desperate sense that our very survival is at stake. We lose touch with the real moments of grace and the real blessings of our life. We forget that things really do get better sometimes, that people can be generous and heroic, and that we know some of them. In fact, in our finer moments we *are* them. For all of our struggles, can anyone really doubt the progress we have made over the last couple of centuries in America to extend the protections of life, liberty, and the pursuit of happiness to more and more people?

The next time you find yourself feeling the effects of "splatterscreen," remember Jesus' proclamation in the book of Revelation: "See, I make all things new!" This includes, of course, the constant reshaping of our hearts and minds by grace. Also reflect on the words of Mother Teresa: "It is not how much we do that matters. It is how much love we put in the doing."

It is wrong to think that God expects any one of us to change the world by ourselves. Yet it is equally wrong to think that any one of us is exempt from being fully immersed in the world. Jesus is fully immersed in the world and that is where he needs his disciples to be. Start small and simple. Notice the deadly sin that seems to have a hold of you the most and take it to prayer. Perhaps begin this way: "Lord, how does this sin prevent me from recognizing the size of the neighborhood and my place and responsibility in it? What would I need to do to begin to overcome this?"

In his autobiography, *The Seven Storey Mountain,* Thomas Merton writes: "In reforming His image in souls distorted and half destroyed by evil and disorder, God makes the works of His wisdom and love all the more strikingly beautiful by reason of the contrast with the surroundings in which He does not disdain to operate." Just as it is an illusion that anyone of us is irredeemable, so is the belief that any social situation is irredeemable. Together, aided by the Spirit and the social justice teaching of the Church, let us go out and explore the global neighborhood.

I hear it's a great place to live.

APPENDIX

THE MAJOR SOCIAL ENCYCLICALS OF THE CATHOLIC CHURCH

Rerum Novarum • Pope Leo XIII, 1891

Quadragesimo Anno • Pope Pius XI, 1931

Mater et Magisra • Pope John XXIII, 1961

Pacem in Terris • Pope John XXIII, 1963

Populorum Progressio • Pope Paul VI, 1967

Octogesima Adveniens • Pope Paul VI, 1971

Laborem Exercens • Pope John Paul II, 1981

Solicidudo Rei Socialis • Pope John Paul II, 1987

Centesimus Annus • Pope John Paul II, 1991

Evangelium Vitae • Pope John Paul II, 1995

Caritas in Veritate • Pope Benedict XVI, 2009

Evangelii Gaudium • Pope Francis, 2013

Laudato Si' • Pope Francis, 2015

To gain a more complete perspective on the social justice teaching of the Church all in one place, read *The Compendium of the Social Doctrine of the Church*, available, as are all these encyclicals, at www.vatican.va.

SOCIAL DOCUMENTS FROM THE SECOND VATICAN COUNCIL

Dignitatis Humanae • 1965

Gaudium et Spes • 1965

TWO LANDMARK SOCIAL ENCYCLICALS BY THE UNITED STATES BISHOPS

The Challenge of Peace • 1983

Economic Justice for All • 1986

For more information on any of the above documents, see www.usccb.org, www.vatican.va or www.catholicsocialteaching.org.uk.